Racist? Really? Let's Do Better, Folks!

Erica Berg & Peter Berg

WHITE TULIP PRESS

FLORIDA

© 2023 by Erica Berg and Peter Berg

All rights reserved. No part of this book may be reproduced or used in any manner without the express written permission of the publisher except for the use of brief quotations in a book review.

Names, characters, businesses, places, events, and incidents are either products of the author's imagination or used in a fictitious manner. Any resemblance to actual persons, living or dead, or actual events is purely coincidental.

This book is designed to provide entertaining and informative material. It is sold with the understanding that the author and publisher are not engaged in rendering legal, financial, or other professional services by providing this book. The author and publisher disclaim any liability, loss, or risk taken by individuals who directly or indirectly act on the information contained herein.

Published by White Tulip Press

First Edition: June 2023

Proudly Printed in the United States of America

ISBN: 979-8398013-67-2

Cover design by Kate Cummings

TABLE OF CONTENTS

Foreword

Ladies and gentlemen, let's get one thing straight right off the bat. This isn't your typical, politically correct, "let's all hold hands and sing Kumbaya" book about racism. No, sir! This is "Racist? Really? Let's Do Better, Folks!" - a no-holds-barred, in-your-face, laugh-out-loud while you cringe and reflect kind of book.

Why? Well, because it's high time we talked about this. Racism, folks, it's everywhere. And it's not a terrific thing, let me tell you. We're in the 21st century, yet we still can't seem to get over the color of each other's skin. It's like we're stuck in a traffic jam of prejudice, honking our horns, but not moving an inch. Sad, isn't it?

Now, let me make one thing clear. This book, it's not written to point fingers, cause offense, or tell you that you're a terrible person. Not at all! It's written in the language of humor, wit, and unabashed honesty. It's designed to hold up a mirror, a mirror with a touch of that Trumpian audacity, you know?

If you're a white person, like me, you might be thinking, "Hey, I'm not racist! I have a black friend!" Well, good for you, but that doesn't mean there isn't more to learn or that you're not unintentionally contributing to systemic racism. There, I said it!

So, what can you expect from this book? Well, we'll explore what racism really is, debunk stereotypes, face privilege head-on, and learn the art of empathy. We'll also explore how to respond when we encounter racism, both in others and within ourselves.

What you're about to embark on is a journey. A journey that's going to be uncomfortable at times, it's going to make you squirm in your seat, laugh out loud, and maybe even tear up a bit. But remember, the best journeys are the ones that change us. And folks, it's time for some change!

As the great Donald J. Trump would say, "We're going to make America great for EVERYONE, folks!" That's the spirit we're starting this journey with. Not division, not anger, but unity and understanding. Because at the end of the day, aren't we all just trying to make it in this world?

So, buckle up, brace yourself, and let's dive into the fantastic journey of "Racist? Really? Let's Do Better, Folks!" Because folks, we can do better. We HAVE to do better. And it starts right here, right now. With you. With me. Together.

Onward we go!

Chapter 1: "Let's Make America Great for EVERYONE, Again!"

Welcome, folks, to the first stop of our journey. Now, I've got a question for you. What makes America great? Is it the liberty? The opportunities? The hot dogs? Maybe. But let's agree on something right now - the greatness of America lies in its diversity. It's the vibrant, colorful tapestry of cultures, languages, and traditions. However, there's an ugly stain on this tapestry, and it's called racism.

Now, what is racism? Some people, they think racism is just calling someone a bad name, refusing to sit next to them on the bus, or not hiring them because of their skin color. But let me tell you, folks, it's more than that. It's systemic. It's institutional. It's that nasty, grating sound in the background of our everyday lives that we've somehow become accustomed to. It's like a bad tune playing on repeat. And it's time to change the track.

Racism, you see, is a belief system. It's the idea that certain races are superior to others, and that's just ridiculous, isn't it? I mean, come on, we're all human! We all bleed red, don't we? But here's where it gets really complex. Racism isn't just about individuals and their beliefs, it's ingrained in our institutions. It's in our schools, our workplaces, our neighborhoods, and even our legal systems.

"But how did we get here?" I hear you ask. Well, racism has its roots in history, in slavery, colonialism, and the idea that white people were the "master race." It's a sad part of our past, but denying it won't make it go away. And though we've made some progress, we've still got a long way to go.

This brings us to a crucial point - white people, like you and me, we've got a role to play. It's easy to say, "I'm not racist, so it's not my problem." But that's where we're wrong. Racism IS our problem, and it's high time we stepped up and did something about it.

It's about recognizing that we benefit from a system that's rigged in our favor, whether we asked for it or not. It's about learning to listen to the experiences of people of color without getting defensive. It's about educating ourselves, questioning our biases, and challenging our prejudices.

Sounds tough, doesn't it? But remember, nobody said this journey was going to be easy. But it's necessary. Because if we truly want to make America great for EVERYONE, we've got to tackle racism head-on. And it starts by acknowledging it, understanding it, and actively working against it.

So folks, let's roll up our sleeves and dive right in. Because an inclusive America, a truly great America, isn't just a dream. It's a possibility, and it's up to us to make it a reality.

Stay tuned for Chapter 2, where we'll be taking a deep dive into the concept of white privilege. It's going to be a bumpy ride, but trust me, it's one worth taking. Let's do better, folks! Because together, we CAN make America great for EVERYONE, again!

Chapter 2: "Unmasking Privilege: A Fantastic Journey"

Well, here we are, folks, Chapter 2. And let me tell you, this is going to be big, really big! We're about to dive into the murky waters of white privilege. Now, I know what some of you are thinking, "White privilege? Not me, I've worked hard for everything I've got!" Hold that thought, folks, we'll get to that.

First things first, let's define what we're talking about here. White privilege is like an invisible package of unearned benefits that people who look like me - and probably you - get. It's like a VIP pass, folks. It gives you an advantage, a head start, a leg up in society.

Now, I'm not saying that if you're white, you've never struggled, or you haven't worked hard. No, not at all. What I am saying, is that your skin color hasn't been a hurdle in your life. You might have had to climb mountains, sure, but you weren't also fighting against the tide of racial bias.

"But how does this privilege show up?" you ask. Great question! Here's how: it's when you walk into a store and don't get followed around by suspicious eyes. It's when you get pulled over by the police, and you're not fearing for your life. It's when you apply for a job, and your name doesn't get your application thrown in the bin.

You see, white privilege is like the air we breathe - it's everywhere, but we just don't notice it. We take it for granted. We don't realize that for people of color, the story's different, and not in a good way. They're fighting against systems that have been stacked against them, right from the start.

But here's the deal, recognizing your privilege doesn't mean feeling guilty or ashamed. It's not about blame, folks. It's about understanding that we've got an unfair advantage and using that to create change. We've got to use our privilege to level the playing field, to speak up for those who've been marginalized and silenced.

It's like this, folks: if you see someone struggling to open a door because they're carrying a heavy load, wouldn't you help them out? Of course, you would! That's what good people do. It's the same with privilege. We've got to help dismantle the barriers that are holding others back.

Now, I understand, coming to terms with your privilege isn't easy. It's uncomfortable. It's like realizing you've had spinach stuck in your teeth all day - it's embarrassing, and you wonder why no one told you sooner. But that's okay, folks. It's never too late to learn, to grow, and to do better.

Remember, privilege isn't about what you've done, or haven't done. It's about what society allows you to do based on the color of your skin. So, folks, let's unmask privilege, let's acknowledge it, let's use it for good. Because, in the words of the great Donald J. Trump, "together, we can make America great for EVERYONE, again!"

Up next, we're going to dive into the art of the fail, why racism isn't smart, and why we need to do better. You won't want to miss it, believe me!

Chapter 3: "The Art of the Fail: Why Racism Isn't Smart"

Alright, folks, onto Chapter 3. Now, I have built quite a few things in my time, won some, lost some, but I've learned a thing or two about failure. Let me tell you, racism, it's a big fat failure, a disaster! It's like trying to build a skyscraper with no foundation - it just won't stand.

You might be wondering, "Why is racism a fail?" Good question. Racism, it's like a poison. It seeps into every nook and cranny of society, causing harm, causing damage, and let me tell you, it's not a pretty sight.

Firstly, it harms individuals. Imagine always being seen as a stereotype, never just as yourself. Always being the punchline, never the main character. It's exhausting, folks. It chips away at people's self-esteem, their mental health, their potential. It's like being in a race, but you're carrying a hundred-pound weight on your back. It's not fair, and it's not smart.

But it doesn't stop there. Racism is bad for society too. It divides us, fosters hatred and misunderstanding, and let's not forget, it's just plain wrong. It's like trying to sail a ship with a hole in the hull - you're not going to get very far.

And here's something that will blow your mind: Racism is bad for the economy too! That's right, folks, it's true. When people are discriminated against, when they're not given the same opportunities, we're wasting talent. We're leaving money on the table. And no smart businessperson would do that, right?

Now, let's bust some myths. Some folks think that racism is natural, that it's part of human nature. But that's fake news, folks! Racism is learned, not innate. We're not born with it, we pick it up from society, from the media, from the people around us. And anything learned can be unlearned. Remember that.

Another myth? "I don't see color, so I can't be racist." Now, that's like saying, "I don't see the sun, so it must be night." Not seeing color doesn't mean racism disappears. It just means you're ignoring the problem, and let me tell you, folks, that's not the solution.

Here's the deal. Racism isn't smart. It's not clever, it's not useful, it's not beneficial. It's a colossal fail. And if we want to make America great for EVERYONE, we've got to acknowledge that. We've got to face up to the harm that racism causes, the division it fosters, and we've got to say, "Enough is enough!"

Coming up next, we're going to tackle some fake news of our own. Get ready to debunk racist stereotypes, because folks, it's time to separate fact from fiction! You won't want to miss it, believe me!

Chapter 4: "That's Fake News: Debunking Racist Stereotypes"

Welcome to Chapter 4, folks! Now, if there's one thing I know a thing or two about, it's fake news. And let me tell you, when it comes to racism, there's a whole lot of it flying around. Racist stereotypes, they're the worst kind of fake news. They're false, they're harmful, and it's about time we debunked them.

First up, let's talk about the stereotype that people of color are lazy. Now, this one is just ridiculous, folks. Lazy? Have you ever seen the work ethic of immigrants, working multiple jobs, striving for a better life for their families? I've seen it, and let me tell you, it's impressive. It's admirable. Laziness is not a racial trait, it's an individual one, and it can be found in any race. So, let's trash this stereotype, once and for all.

Next, there's the idea that all people of color are dangerous or criminal. Now, folks, that's just absurd. Crime, it's not a racial trait. It's about socioeconomic conditions, about opportunities, or the lack thereof. And let's not forget, white-collar crime, it's a thing, and it's not committed by people of color living in inner cities. It's committed by white folks in suits and ties. So, this stereotype, it's a big fat lie, and it's time we acknowledged that.

Then there's the myth that people of color are not as intelligent as white folks. Folks, this one is not only false, it's offensive. Intelligence is not determined by skin color. It's about access to quality education, it's about opportunities. Remember, we've had people of color excel in every field, from science to literature, from sports to politics. So, this stereotype, it's not just fake news, it's an insult to human dignity.

Here's the bottom line, folks: Stereotypes, they're a form of lazy thinking. They're about putting people into boxes based on the color of their skin, and that's just not right. It's not fair, and it's not smart.

Stereotypes dehumanize people, they reduce them to one-dimensional caricatures, and they foster misunderstanding and fear. And remember, fear is the breeding ground for hate.

So, folks, let's pledge to do better. Let's pledge to question our biases, to challenge the stereotypes we've unconsciously absorbed. Let's pledge to see people as individuals, not as stereotypes. Because at the end of the day, aren't we all just human beings, trying to make our way in the world?

Coming up next, we're going to learn how to be allies. It's a big word, folks, but don't worry, we'll break it down. You won't want to miss it, believe me!

Chapter 6: "You're Fired, Prejudice!"

Alright, folks, we've made it to Chapter 6, and let me tell you, it's a good one. We're going to be dealing with a phrase I've used more than a few times in my life, "You're fired!" But this time, it's not about bad employees, it's about prejudice. It's time to show it the door, and here's how.

First up, we need to know our enemy. Now, prejudice, it's sneaky. It disguises itself as harmless jokes, as unconscious bias, as 'just the way things are'. But make no mistake, folks, prejudice is harmful. It's a barrier to equality, and it needs to be shown the door.

The first step in fighting prejudice is to recognize it. You might be thinking, "I'm not prejudiced!" But folks, prejudice is like a weed. It grows in the unexamined corners of our minds, and it spreads if left unchecked. It's time to do some self-reflection, to question our beliefs and assumptions, and to acknowledge our biases.

Next, it's about education. Remember, folks, knowledge is power. Read books by authors of different races, watch movies that challenge your perspective, engage in conversations with people from different backgrounds. Educate yourself about other cultures, their histories, their struggles, their triumphs. When we understand each other, prejudice loses its power.

Now, here's the big one: calling out prejudice. This one's tough, folks. It's uncomfortable, but it's necessary. If you hear a racist joke, don't laugh. If you see someone being discriminated against, speak up. If you witness racial profiling, call it out. Silence, folks, it's complicity. Let's use our voices to stand up against prejudice.

And finally, we need to listen. When people of color talk about their experiences with racism, don't get defensive, don't try to downplay their experiences. Listen, empathize, and understand. Remember, folks, their reality might be different from yours, and that's okay. It's not about guilt, it's about understanding.

Now, I know this is a lot. It's not easy. But remember, folks, anything worth doing isn't easy. It's a process, it's a journey. And it's one we need to take if we truly want to make America great for EVERYONE.

Coming up in our next chapter, we're going to tackle a big question: "What is systemic racism?" It's a term you've probably heard a lot, but what does it really mean? Stay tuned, folks, because we're about to take a deep dive into the murky waters of systemic racism. You won't want to miss it, believe me!

Chapter 7: "Negotiating with Ignorance: Tips to Educate the Misinformed"

Welcome back, folks! Chapter 7 is here and it's all about dealing with the folks who didn't know they needed this book as much as they do. We've all encountered them - friends, family members, coworkers who hold onto prejudiced views and seem to be stuck in the mud of misinformation. Let's talk about how we can help pull them out.

First off, you gotta know: Patience is key. I've done my fair share of negotiating, folks, and I can tell you it's not about fast results. It's a game of chess, not checkers. Remember, changing someone's mindset isn't about winning a debate; it's about planting a seed and nurturing its growth.

Next up, listening. Now, I know what you're thinking, "Why should I listen to someone who's spouting prejudiced views?" Here's the thing, folks. Listening doesn't mean agreeing. It's about understanding where they're coming from. And when people feel heard, they're more likely to listen in return.

Now, onto the third point: Educate with empathy. If you start by telling people they're wrong, they'll shut down faster than a failed casino.

Instead, share what you've learned. Talk about the books you've read, the documentaries you've watched, the conversations you've had. Approach them with empathy, not with judgment.

And here's a crucial one, folks: Ask questions. Don't just challenge their views, make them examine them. When people have to explain their prejudices, they often start to see the holes in their thinking. It's not about gotcha questions, folks. It's about making them see the bigger picture.

Finally, and this one's important, folks: Know when to walk away. Some folks, they're not ready to change, not yet. And that's okay. You've planted a seed, and that's enough. Remember, you can't force someone to see the truth, but you can make sure it's available to them when they're ready.

I won't lie to you, folks, it's a tough road. It's like trying to turn a cruise ship on a dime - it's not going to happen quickly. But every journey starts with a single step, and every change starts with a single voice. So let's get out there, folks, and start negotiating with ignorance.

In our next chapter, we're going to take a deep dive into the thorny issue of systemic racism. It's a big topic, folks, but we'll break it down, piece by piece. You won't want to miss it, believe me!

Chapter 8: "The Big Comeback: Building an Inclusive Community"

Welcome back to Chapter 8, folks! And I have to say, this one's going to be a hit, trust me. We're talking about making the big comeback, fighting back against racism by building inclusive communities. Let's roll up our sleeves and get to work.

First, let's be clear, diversity isn't a threat, folks, it's an asset. Think about it. When you have people from different backgrounds, with different experiences, you get a broader range of ideas, a richer culture, and a stronger community. It's like a potluck, folks. The more variety you have, the better the feast.

So, how do we build these inclusive communities? Let me share some success stories, some fantastic examples from across our great country.

Let's start with the town of Harmony, Minnesota. Now, Harmony, they're doing something right. They've created a Diversity and Inclusion Committee that's focused on promoting cultural understanding and appreciation. They host cultural events, sponsor language classes, even started a mentorship program for newcomers. It's a real melting pot, folks, and it's working.

Then there's the city of Unity, Oregon. Unity, they're all about education. They've revamped their school curriculum to include the history and contributions of various racial and ethnic groups. It's about giving kids a complete education, folks, one that reflects the diversity of our nation.

And let's not forget about the Community of Welcome in Kentucky. This community, they're tackling prejudice head-on. They host 'Living Library' events, where people can 'check out' individuals from different backgrounds for a chat. It's about breaking down barriers, folks, and it's making a difference.

But here's the thing. Building an inclusive community isn't just about grand gestures, it's about everyday actions. It's about standing up against prejudice, even when it's uncomfortable. It's about educating ourselves and others. It's about celebrating our differences, not just tolerating them.

So here's my challenge to you, folks. Let's be the change we want to see in our communities. Let's start the conversation about race, even if it's difficult. Let's be allies, advocates, and friends. Because together, we can make America a place where everyone is truly free.

In the next chapter, we'll be putting everything we've learned into action. We're talking practical, hands-on strategies for fighting racism in our everyday lives. You won't want to miss it, believe me!

Conclusion: "Let's Do Better, Folks!"

And here we are, folks, at the end of our journey. It's been quite a ride, hasn't it? We've laughed, we've learned, and hopefully, we've taken a good hard look at ourselves and the world around us. Now it's time for the big finish, so let's dive right in.

If there's one thing we've learned, it's this: Racism, it's not a 'them' problem, it's an 'us' problem. It's not just about the bad apples, folks. It's about the tree, the soil, the whole orchard. And if we want to harvest the fruits of equality and justice, we need to get our hands dirty.

But here's the good news: We have the power to make a difference. Each and every one of us. It's not about grand gestures, folks. It's about the small choices we make every day. It's about questioning our assumptions, checking our biases, standing up against injustice.

It's about education, folks. It's about understanding the history of racism, the systemic barriers that people of color face, the harmful stereotypes that we've unconsciously absorbed. It's about educating ourselves, our friends, our families. Because knowledge, folks, it's a powerful tool. And it's a tool we all have access to.

And finally, it's about empathy. It's about recognizing that we're all human beings, folks, all deserving of respect and dignity. It's about understanding that someone else's struggle might be different from ours, but it's no less important.

So here's my challenge to you, folks. Let's do better. Let's be better. Let's recognize the part we've played in perpetuating racism, and let's take steps to rectify it. Let's be the change we want to see in the world.

Because at the end of the day, folks, it's not about guilt or blame. It's about responsibility. It's about recognizing that we all have a role to play in fighting racism, and it's about stepping up to the plate.

So, folks, it's been a pleasure. I hope this book has opened your eyes, made you think, made you laugh. And most of all, I hope it's inspired you to make a difference. Because remember, we're all in this together, folks. And together, we can make America great for EVERYONE.

Now, get out there and start making a difference, folks. Because I believe in you, and I know you can do it. You're the best, trust me!

Until next time, folks. It's been a blast. Keep fighting the good fight. You won't want to miss what comes next, believe me!

Page 29